Humble Bumbles®

Baby Journal

A keepsake journal for baby's first three years.

for our littlest angel.

All that is worth cherishing begins
in the heart, not the head.
~ Suzanne Chapin

Humble Bumbles®

www.humblebumbles.com

written, illustrated and designed
by Amy Meyer Allen

ISBN 13: 978-1-887169-31-8
Printed in China

table of contents...

First steps
page 64

Birth photo
Page 21

Here we grow...
page 52

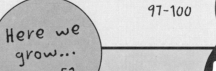

place sonogram photo here

BEFORE YOU WERE BORN

Diapers and clothing
and toys... oh my!

Preparing for your arrival
how quickly time goes by.

daddy's family tree

great grandpa

great grandpa

great grandma

great grandma

Mario Elia
grandpa (nonno)

Antonietta Elia
grandma (nonna)

Petro Elia
daddy

let me tell you about the birds

8

mommy's family tree

Costantino Santilli
great grandpa (bisnonno)

Luigi Saviganano
great grandpa (bisnono)

Francesca
great grandma (bisnonna)

Lucia DeProspo
great grandma (bisnonna)

Domenico Santilli
grandpa (nonno)

Guiseppina Santilli
grandma (nonna)

Lucia Santilli
MOMMY

and the bees...

9

all about mommy...

Full given name: _Lucia Francesca Santilli_

Birth date: _May 28th 1974_

Where she was born: _Oshawa Ontario ; Canada_

Eye color: _dark brown_

Hair color: _dark brown_

Distinguishing Features: _dark_

Age when she met daddy: _30 yrs old_

Treasured childhood memories: _being with family -_
cousins, siblings

What she wanted to be when she grew up: _doctor,_
lawyer, realestate, hairdresser

Favorite things to do: _Shop and talk_

Sugar and spice and everything nice, that's what little girls are made of.

place photo of mommy on this page

all about daddy...

Full given name: _____

Birth date: _____

Where he was born: _____

Eye color: _____

Hair color: _____

Distinguishing features: _____

Age when he met mommy: _____

Treasured childhood memories: _____

_____

_____

_____

What he wanted to be when he grew up: _____

_____

_____

Favorite things to do: _____

_____

Snips and snails and puppy dog tails, that's what little boys are made of.

place photo of daddy on this page

13

Date: _____

Host(s): _____

Theme: _____

_____

People who attended: _____

_____

_____

_____

_____

_____

_____

Favorite gifts received: _____

_____

_____

_____

_____

_____

I will send down showers in season; there will be
showers of blessing. ~ Ezekiel 34:26

place baby shower photo
or invitation here

getting ready...

Nickname before you were born: _____

Choosing your name: _____
_____

What your name means: _____
_____

Color and theme of your room: _____
_____
_____

Thoughts or stories about getting ready: _____
_____
_____
_____
_____
_____
_____
_____
_____

Babies are always more trouble than you thought –
and more wonderful. ~ Charles Osgood

place photo of baby's room here

a few thoughts about before you were born...

_____

_____

_____

_____

_____

_____

_____

_____

_____

_____

_____

_____

_____

_____

~ signed and dated

Before I formed you in the womb I knew you,
before you were born I set you apart... ~ Jeremiah 1:5

THE BIG DAY IS HERE!

The day has arrived;
it's finally here!

The day you were born
filled with hope and good cheer!

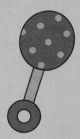

all about baby...

Where were you born: _____

Birth date: _____

How long labor lasted: _____

Time of delivery: _____

Weight: _____

Length: _____

Eye color: _____

Hair color: _____

Doctor's name: _____

How we welcomed you into the world: _____

_____

_____

_____

_____

_____

_____

A baby is God's way of saying the world must go on.
~ Carl Sandburg

place newborn photo here

hospital bracelet or other keepsakes

so many visitors...

First people to hold you: _____
_____
_____
_____
_____
_____

Some of their comments: _____
_____
_____
_____
_____

Cute things you did: _____
_____
_____
_____

A baby is born with a need to be loved and never
outgrows it. ~ Frank A. Clark

tiny fingers...

baby's hand prints

_____

date

Children are the hands by which we take hold of heaven.
~ Henry Ward Beecher

tiny toes...

baby's foot prints

_____
date

If you want children to keep their feet on the ground,
put some responsibility on their shoulders. ~ Abigail Van Buren

25

newborn photo with mommy...

place photo with mommy on this page

place photo with daddy on this page

thoughts on the day of your birth...

_____
_____
_____
_____
_____
_____
_____
_____
_____
_____
_____
_____
_____
_____
~ signed and dated

You.

A longing fulfilled is sweet to the soul... ~ Proverbs 13:19

BRINGING YOU HOME

Oh baby of ours
we welcome you home.

A precious new life
to call our own.

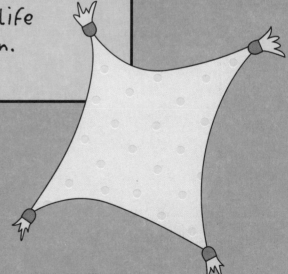

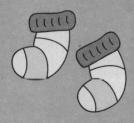

home is where the heart is...

Your first address: _____

_____

How your siblings reacted: _____

_____

_____

Who came to visit: _____

_____

What your visitors said about you: _____

_____

_____

Your temperament: _____

_____

How much you slept: _____

_____

How much you ate: _____

_____

Where we love is home – home that our feet may leave,
but not our hearts. ~ Oliver Wendell Holmes Sr.

place homecoming photo here

31

President of the United States: _____

Big news of the day: _____

_____

_____

_____

_____

Biggest toy fad: _____

_____

Movies: _____

_____

Hit songs: _____

_____

Musical groups: _____

_____

Television shows: _____

_____

We do not inherit this land from our ancestors;
we borrow it from our children. ~ Haida Indian Saying

more about your world...

Actors and actresses: _____

_____

Sports figures: _____

_____

Best-selling books: _____

_____

Fashion trends: _____

_____

THE PRICE OF THINGS:

Gasoline: _____

Milk: _____

Diapers: _____

Postage stamp: _____

Other: _____

_____

_____

Do not confine your children to your own learning,
for they were born in another time. ~ Chinese Proverb

33

announcing your arrival...

How we told the world: _____
_____
_____
_____

Your very own website: _____
_____

What the neighbors said: _____
_____
_____

What your pet(s) thought about you: _____
_____
_____

Who bragged about you the most: _____
_____
_____
_____

Babies are such a nice way to start people. ~ Don Herald

place birth announcement here

Christening, dedication, bris or special commemoration:

_____

_____

Date: _____

Where: _____

_____

What you wore: _____

_____

Who attended: _____

_____

_____

_____

_____

_____

_____

...children are a reward from Him. ~ Psalm 127:3

place celebration photo here

thoughts on the first few weeks of your life...

_____

_____

_____

_____

_____

_____

_____

_____

_____

_____

_____

_____

_____

_____

~ signed and dated

Pleasant words are a honeycomb, sweet to the soul and healing to the bones.
~ Proverbs 16:24

more thoughts...

_____
_____
_____
_____
_____
_____
_____
_____
_____
_____
_____
_____
_____
_____
~ signed and dated

a little
note

thoughts on bringing you home...

_____
_____
_____
_____
_____
_____
_____
_____
_____
_____
_____
_____
_____

~ signed and dated

You.

Home is where one starts from. ~ T.S. Eliot

YOUR FAVORITE THINGS

Snuggly warm blankets
and butterfly kisses.

Singing you to sleep
with sweet dream wishes.

lullaby baby...

a few of your favorite things...

Favorite cuddle object: _____
_____

Favorite security object: _____
_____

Favorite song or lullaby: _____
_____

Favorite time to eat: _____
_____

Favorite time to sleep: _____
_____

Favorite person to hold you: _____
_____

Favorite way to be held: _____
_____

Other favorites: _____
_____

Each day of our lives we make deposits in the
memory banks of our children. ~ Charles R. Swindoll

more of your favorite things...

Favorite outfit: _____
_____

Favorite place to visit: _____
_____

Favorite thing to do: _____
_____

Favorite book: _____
_____

Favorite pet: _____
_____

Favorite friends: _____
_____

Favorite games: _____
_____

Other favorites: _____
_____

HONEY

Quickly changed diapers
with fresh baby powder;
Lullabies sung in a whisper, no louder;
Butterfly kisses with soft tickly wings;
These are a few of my favorite things.

The best and most beautiful things in the world cannot be seen
or even touched. They must be felt with the heart.
~ Helen Keller

place photo of baby
with favorite toy here

Mommy's mommy and daddy: _____

_____

What they have to say about you: _____

_____

_____

_____

Daddy's mommy and daddy: _____

_____

What they have to say about you: _____

_____

_____

_____

Great-grandparents: _____

_____

Who has the most pictures of you: _____

_____

Grandchildren are God's way of compensating
us for growing old. ~ Mary H. Waldrip

FREE
HUGS

place photo with grandparents
on this page

favorite family moments...

Aunts and uncles: _____
_____

What they have to say about you: _____
_____
_____
_____

Cousins: _____
_____

What they have to say about you: _____
_____
_____
_____

Funny stories: _____
_____
_____
_____

Love is patient, love is kind.
~ 1 Corinthians 13:4

place photo with relatives
on this page

thinking of your favorite things...

_____

_____

_____

_____

_____

_____

_____

_____

_____

_____

_____

_____

_____

~ signed and dated

You.

Life, love and laughter - what priceless gifts
to give our children. ~ Phyllis Dryden

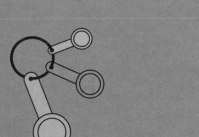

OH HOW YOU GROW!

An ounce then a pound
you're growing so fast.

Oh how I wish for your
baby days to last.

the first six months go so fast...

MONTH ONE:

Date: _____ Weight: _____ Length: _____

Comments: _____

MONTH TWO:

Date: _____ Weight: _____ Length: _____

Comments: _____

MONTH THREE:

Date: _____ Weight: _____ Length: _____

Comments: _____

MONTH FOUR:

Date: _____ Weight: _____ Length: _____

Comments: _____

MONTH FIVE:

Date: _____ Weight: _____ Length: _____

Comments: _____

MONTH SIX:

Date: _____ Weight: _____ Length: _____

Comments: _____

There are two lasting bequests we can give our children.
One is roots. The other is wings. ~ Hodding Carter, Jr.

place a photo of baby
between the ages of 1-6 months

try to make each moment last...

MONTH SEVEN:

Date: _____ Weight: _____ Length: _____

Comments: _____

MONTH EIGHT:

Date: _____ Weight: _____ Length: _____

Comments: _____

MONTH NINE:

Date: _____ Weight: _____ Length: _____

Comments: _____

MONTH TEN:

Date: _____ Weight: _____ Length: _____

Comments: _____

MONTH ELEVEN:

Date: _____ Weight: _____ Length: _____

Comments: _____

MONTH TWELVE:

Date: _____ Weight: _____ Length: _____

Comments: _____

The potential possibilities of any child are the most intriguing and stimulating in all creation. ~ Ray L. Wilbur

place a photo of baby
between the ages of 7-12 months

_____

_____

_____

_____

_____

_____

_____

_____

_____

_____

_____

_____

_____

_____

~ signed and dated

You.

Every hour of the day and night is an
unspeakably perfect miracle. ~ Walt Whitman

A FEW OF YOUR FIRSTS

The first time you smiled
I remember so well.

With all your first times
there's a story to tell!

mama...dada...

THE FIRST TIME YOU:

Smiled: _____

Laughed: _____

Held your head up: _____

Rolled over: _____

Sat up: _____

Held a bottle: _____

Waved bye-bye: _____

Crawled: _____

Stood up: _____

Took your first steps: _____

Played peek-a-boo: _____

Slept through the night: _____

Ate baby food: _____

Ate solid food: _____

Fed yourself: _____

A man finds out what is meant by a spitting image
when he tries to feed cereal to his infant. ~ Imogene Fey

THE FIRST TIME YOU:

Said your first word: _____

Said other words: _____

Bathed in bathtub: _____

Went potty: _____

Stopped wearing diapers: _____

Dressed yourself: _____

Said abc's: _____

Sang a song: _____

Danced: _____

Drew a picture: _____

Wrote the alphabet: _____

Made a friend: _____

Took a trip: _____

Talked on the phone: _____

Other firsts: _____

PRIVACY PLEASE!

Children have more need of models than of critics.
~ Carolyn Coats

your very first haircut...

Date: _____

Who cut it: _____

How much was cut: _____

What you thought about it: _____

_____

_____

_____

_____

_____

_____

_____

_____

_____

_____

There's only one pretty child in the world,
and every mother has it. ~ J.C. Bridge

a lock of hair from baby's first haircut

your very first tooth...

Your dentist: _____

Your first visit: _____

What you thought about it: _____

Dates your teeth first appeared:

Upper	Left	Right
1. Central incisor	_____	_____
2. Lateral incisor	_____	_____
3. Cuspid	_____	_____
4. First molar	_____	_____
5. Second molar	_____	_____

Lower	Left	Right
1. Central incisor	_____	_____
2. Lateral incisor	_____	_____
3. Cuspid	_____	_____
4. First molar	_____	_____
5. Second molar	_____	_____

Adam and Eve had many advantages, but the principal one was that they escaped teething. ~ Mark Twain

place photo of baby
with first tooth

your very First steps...

Day you pulled yourself up to standing: _____
_____

Day you First stood on your own: _____
_____

Day you took your First steps: _____
_____
_____
_____

How we celebrated the big moment: _____
_____
_____
_____
_____
_____

Your First pair of real shoes: _____
_____

Remember, we all stumble, every one of us. That's why
it's a comfort to go hand in hand. ~ Emily Kimbrough

place photo of baby
taking first steps

Date: _____

Where we went: _____

_____

How much we had to take: _____

_____

What we did: _____

_____

_____

_____

_____

Who we saw: _____

What they said about you: _____

_____

_____

_____

How long it took: _____

To bring up a child in the way he should go, travel that way
yourself once in a while. ~ Josh Billings

traveling for the first time...

Date: _____

Who you went to see: _____

How we traveled: _____

How much we took with us: _____

_____

_____

What you thought about it: _____

_____

_____

_____

_____

_____

_____

_____

_____

_____

Holiday: _____

What we did: _____

_____

_____

Holiday: _____

What we did: _____

_____

_____

Holiday: _____

What we did: _____

_____

_____

Holiday: _____

What we did: _____

_____

_____

Youth is, after all, just a moment, the spark that you always carry in your heart. ~ Raisa M. Gorbachev

Born free!

place photo of baby
celebrating a holiday

place first drawing here

your very first pet...

First pet's name: _____

What you thought about it: _____

_____

_____

_____

What it thought about you: _____

_____

_____

_____

How you played with it: _____

_____

_____

_____

What you learned from your pet: _____

_____

_____

I have loved you with an everlasting love;
I have drawn you with loving-kindness. ~ Jeremiah 31:3

71

thoughts on some of your firsts...

_____
_____
_____
_____
_____
_____
_____
_____
_____
_____
_____
_____
_____
_____
_____

~ signed and dated

You.

There is a time for everything, and a season for every
activity under heaven... ~ Ecclesiastes 3:1

HAPPY FIRST BIRTHDAY!

Oh my goodness,
where has the time gone?

I can hardly believe
that you're already one!

Theme: _____
_____

How we celebrated: _____
_____

Your cake and what you thought about it: _____
_____

Who attended: Gifts:

_____   _____

_____   _____

_____   _____

_____   _____

_____   _____

_____   _____

_____   _____

_____   _____

Once in a lifetime one should be allowed to have as much
sweetness as one can possibly want and hold. ~ Judith Olney

place birthday party
photo on this page

Height: _____

Weight: _____

You look more and more like: _____
_____

Most used words and phrases: _____
_____
_____
_____

Most amazing things you've learned to do: _____
_____
_____
_____

Things we wish you hadn't learned to do: _____
_____
_____
_____

Children need love, especially when they do not deserve it.
~ Harold Hulbert

one-year-old favorites...

Favorite foods: _____
_____

Favorite books: _____
_____

Favorite activity: _____
_____

Favorite toys: _____
_____

Favorite outfits: _____
_____

Favorite friends: _____
_____

Favorite things to do: _____
_____

Other favorites: _____
_____

You definitely liked: _____

_____

_____

_____

_____

You definitely did not like: _____

_____

_____

Funniest one-year-old stories: _____

_____

_____

_____

_____

_____

_____

_____

_____

It was from you that I first learned to think, to feel,
to imagine, to believe. ~ John Sterling

place one-year-old
photo on this page

thoughts on your first birthday...

~ signed and dated

You.

Thanks be to God for His indescribable gift!
~ 2 Corinthians 9:15

LOOK AT YOU...
YOU TURNED TWO!

You have doubled in age;
nearly doubled in size.

From one year to two,
right before my eyes!

Theme: _____
_____

How we celebrated: _____
_____

Your cake and what you thought about it: _____
_____

Who attended: Gifts:

_____   _____

_____   _____

_____   _____

_____   _____

_____   _____

_____   _____

_____   _____

_____   _____

...everlasting joy will crown their heads.
~ Isaiah 35:10

place birthday party
photo on this page

Height: _____

Weight: _____

You act more and more like: _____
_____

Most used words and phrases: _____
_____
_____
_____

Most amazing things you've learned to do: _____
_____
_____
_____

Things we wish you hadn't learned to do: _____
_____
_____
_____

Every person's life is a fairy tale written by God's fingers.
~ Hans Christian Andersen

two-year-old favorites...

Favorite foods: _____

_____

Favorite books: _____

_____

Favorite games: _____

_____

Favorite toys: _____

_____

Favorite outfits: _____

_____

Favorite friends: _____

_____

Favorite things to do: _____

_____

Other favorites: _____

_____

You liked it when: _____
_____
_____
_____
_____

You couldn't stand it when: _____
_____
_____

Funniest two-year-old stories: _____
_____
_____
_____
_____
_____
_____
_____

Too often we give children answers to remember
rather than problems to solve. ~ Roger Lewin

place two-year-old
photo on this page

thoughts on your second birthday...

_____

_____

_____

_____

_____

_____

_____

_____

_____

_____

_____

_____

_____

_____

~ signed and dated

You.

Don't worry that children never listen to you;
worry that they are always watching you. ~ Robert Fulghum

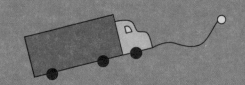

GOLLY GEE...
NOW YOU'RE THREE!

At one you were just beginning,
at two you really did grow.

Now there's just no stopping you,
at three you steal the show!

celebrating your third birthday...

Theme: _____

_____

How we celebrated: _____

_____

Your cake and what you thought about it: _____

_____

Who attended: Gifts:

_____   _____

_____   _____

_____   _____

_____   _____

_____   _____

_____   _____

_____   _____

_____   _____

A happy heart makes the face cheerful...
~ Proverbs 15:13

place birthday party
photo on this page

Height: _____

Weight: _____

You sound more and more like: _____

_____

Most used words and phrases: _____

_____

_____

_____

Most amazing things you've learned to do: _____

_____

_____

_____

Things we wish you hadn't learned to do: _____

_____

_____

_____

Making the decision to have a child is momentous. It is to decide forever
to have your heart go walking around outside your body. ~ Elizabeth Stone

three-year-old favorites...

Favorite foods: _____

_____

Favorite books: _____

_____

Favorite games: _____

_____

Favorite toys: _____

_____

Favorite outfits: _____

_____

Favorite friends: _____

_____

Favorite things to do: _____

_____

Other favorites: _____

_____

You thought highly of: _____

_____

_____

_____

_____

You didn't think much of: _____

_____

_____

Funniest three-year-old stories: _____

_____

_____

_____

_____

_____

_____

_____

Train a child in the way he should go, and when he is old he will not turn from it. ~ Proverbs 22:6

place three-year-old
photo on this page

thoughts on your third birthday...

_____

_____

_____

_____

_____

_____

_____

_____

_____

_____

_____

_____

_____

~ signed and dated

You.

The human heart, at whatever age, opens only to the heart
that opens in return. ~ Maria Edgeworth

LOOKING TOWARD THE FUTURE

It matters not where you go,
or what you plan to do.

Of one thing you can be certain,
our unconditional love for you!

letter from mommy...

_____

_____

_____

_____

_____

_____

_____

_____

_____

_____

_____

_____

_____

_____

~ signed and dated

Being a full-time mother is one of the highest salaried jobs...
since the payment is pure love. ~ Mildred B. Vermont

letter from daddy...

_____

_____

_____

_____

_____

_____

_____

_____

_____

_____

_____

_____

_____

_____

_____

~ signed and dated

The most important thing a father can do for his children
is to love their mother. ~ Theodore M. Hesburgh

Keep reaching for the stars!

for I know the plans I have for you, declares the Lord, plans to
prosper you and not to harm you, plans to give you hope and a future.
~ Jeremiah 29:11